No-Doc & Alternative HELOC Programs

How to Access Home Equity Without Tax Returns or Full Documentation

By Joseph G. Correa

Licensed Mortgage Broker, Finibi Mortgage

Copyright & Legal Notice

First Edition, 2026

Table of Contents

Foreword

For most homeowners, the idea of tapping home equity is immediately paired with anxiety about paperwork, income verification, tax returns, profit-and-loss statements, and invasive financial scrutiny. For self-employed individuals, business owners, investors, and even high-net-worth borrowers with complex finances, that anxiety often turns into outright avoidance. They assume that if their income does not fit neatly into W-2 boxes, their home equity is locked away, unreachable, and irrelevant to their financial future. This belief is one of the most damaging myths in modern lending, and it is exactly why this book exists. Home equity is not reserved for perfect borrowers with perfect paperwork. It is an asset class, and like any asset, it can be leveraged intelligently when you understand the rules that govern it.

Over the last two decades, lending has gone through several massive shifts. The financial crisis created a hyper-conservative environment where income documentation became rigid, formulaic, and often disconnected from real financial strength. At the same time, the American workforce was quietly transforming. Millions of people became independent contractors, entrepreneurs, real estate investors, gig workers, and business owners. Traditional underwriting failed to keep up with this evolution. Today, many of the strongest borrowers on paper appear "unqualified" under old-world guidelines, even though they may have six-figure bank balances, multiple income streams, appreciating real estate, and low risk of default. Book 6 exists to bridge this gap between how people actually earn money and how lenders are willing to recognize it.

As a licensed mortgage broker who works with real borrowers every day, I can tell you something that rarely gets said publicly: there are far more ways to qualify for a HELOC than most banks are willing to advertise. The retail branch down the street is not designed for creativity or nuance. It is designed for volume and uniformity. But the private lending market, non-QM programs, and asset-based structures operate under a completely different philosophy. They look at wealth, not just income. They look at liquidity, not just tax returns. They look at real-world risk, not automated checklists. Once you understand this shift, the entire landscape of home equity opens up in ways that feel almost unfair—until you realize it is simply a different rulebook.

This book is not about shortcuts or deception. It is about using the correct financial lens for your real situation. If you are self-employed, you already know that tax strategy and lending strategy are often in conflict. The same deductions that reduce your tax burden also reduce your qualifying income on paper. Traditional banks punish you for being financially smart. No-doc and alternative HELOC programs correct this imbalance by allowing lenders to evaluate what actually matters: the equity in your home, the stability of your assets, the depth of your reserves, and the overall strength of your financial position. In other words, they measure your ability to repay based on reality, not on outdated templates.

Throughout this series, you have learned that a HELOC is not just a loan—it is a financial tool. In Book 1, you learned how HELOCs really work. In Book 2, you learned how to qualify. In Book 3, you learned how investors scale with them. In Book 4, you learned how self-employed borrowers break through barriers. In Book 5, you learned how credit determines pricing and approval. Now in Book 6, you are going deeper into one of the most powerful areas of modern lending: programs that allow you to access your equity without being forced into full documentation or traditional income verification.

This matters because your home is often your largest store of dormant capital. It sits quietly on your balance sheet, appreciating over time, while inflation eats away at the purchasing power of your cash. When accessed correctly, that equity can be used to consolidate high-interest debt, fund investments, stabilize cash flow, or create entirely new income streams. When accessed incorrectly—or not at all—it remains trapped, even while you struggle with expensive credit cards, business funding constraints, or missed opportunities. The difference between these two outcomes is not luck. It is knowledge.

No-doc and alternative HELOC programs are often misunderstood, sometimes intentionally. Many people think they disappeared after the financial crisis. Others believe they are only for risky borrowers or desperate situations. In reality, these programs are often used by some of the wealthiest and most sophisticated borrowers in the country. Real estate investors, private business owners, doctors, entrepreneurs, and high-net-worth families use them because they value speed, flexibility, and control over their financial structure. They do not want their entire financial life audited just to move capital from one asset to another. They want efficiency—and that is exactly what these programs provide.

This book will show you how these programs actually work, who they are designed for, and how lenders evaluate risk when tax returns are not the centerpiece of the file. You will learn how asset-based underwriting functions, how bank statement programs differ from stated income models, how DSCR-style logic is applied to HELOCs, and how loan-to-value ratios replace income ratios in certain structures. More importantly, you will learn how to position yourself correctly so that lenders see you as a low-risk, high-quality borrower, even without traditional documentation.

If you have ever been told "no" by a bank despite having strong assets, this book is for you. If you have income that fluctuates, comes from multiple sources, or is structured through a business, this book is for you. If you are an investor who understands leverage but hates paperwork, this book is for you. And if you simply want access to your own money without being treated like a suspect, this book is definitely for you.

Home equity is not about borrowing—it is about capital management. The same wealthy families that have controlled capital for generations understand this principle deeply. They use lines of credit to move money strategically, not emotionally. They borrow against assets, not income. They allow their wealth to stay invested while they deploy liquidity where it creates the highest return. No-doc and alternative HELOC programs are one of the most direct ways everyday homeowners can begin using the same financial architecture that the wealthy have always used.

As you read this book, keep one important truth in mind: the lending system is not designed to serve everyone equally, but it does have doors that can be opened if you know where to look.

This book gives you the map. It will not only show you what programs exist, but how to approach them intelligently, ethically, and strategically so that you can unlock the equity you have already earned.

By the time you finish this book, you will no longer see tax returns as the gatekeeper to your financial future. You will see your home, your assets, and your financial structure as the real foundation of your borrowing power. And once you understand that, your relationship with money, credit, and opportunity will never be the same.

Chapter 1

The New Era of No-Doc & Alternative HELOC Lending

The traditional mortgage and home equity system was designed for a world that no longer exists. It was built for employees who received steady paychecks, a single W-2, and predictable career paths. Today, millions of financially strong homeowners earn income from businesses, real estate, consulting, online platforms, investments, or multiple sources that do not fit neatly into a tax return. Yet most banks still rely on tax documents as their primary tool for measuring risk. This disconnect is the single biggest reason so many qualified homeowners are wrongly denied access to their own equity. Understanding this shift is the foundation of mastering no-doc and alternative HELOC programs.

At its core, lending is about one thing: risk. A lender does not care how you earn money as much as whether they will get paid back. Traditional underwriting uses income documents because they are easy to verify and standardize. But income is only one way to measure risk. Assets, equity, liquidity, and property value are often much stronger indicators of repayment. If someone owns a $1 million home with a small mortgage and has hundreds of thousands in reserves, the risk of default is extremely low, even if their tax returns show little taxable income. Alternative HELOC programs are designed around this more intelligent view of risk.

No-doc and alternative documentation HELOCs fall under what the industry calls non-QM lending. Non-QM does not mean risky or subprime. It simply means "non-qualified mortgage," which refers to loans that do not follow rigid government-backed underwriting formulas. These programs exist specifically to serve borrowers with real financial strength but nontraditional income. Instead of forcing a borrower into a one-size-fits-all model, non-QM lenders look at the total financial picture. This includes home equity, loan-to-value, cash reserves, asset statements, rent rolls, and real-world cash flow.

One of the most important concepts in no-doc HELOC lending is loan-to-value, often called LTV. LTV measures how much of the home's value is being borrowed. The lower the LTV, the lower the risk to the lender. If a home is worth $500,000 and the total debt against it is $250,000, the LTV is 50 percent. That means there is a huge equity cushion protecting the lender. In many no-doc HELOC programs, LTV replaces income as the primary risk control. A borrower with strong equity can often qualify even if they show very little taxable income. Another critical factor is liquidity. Liquidity means how much accessible cash or assets a borrower has after closing. Lenders like to see that even if income slows down, the borrower has enough reserves to continue making payments. This could be money in bank accounts, investment accounts, retirement funds, or other liquid assets. Many alternative HELOC programs will require six to twelve months of reserves, which dramatically lowers default risk. In these cases, the lender is not asking, "How much do you earn?" They are asking, "How long could you keep paying even if income stopped?"

Some alternative HELOC programs use bank statements instead of tax returns. Instead of verifying taxable income, the lender analyzes deposits going into the borrower's accounts. This is far more accurate for business owners, contractors, and investors. If someone deposits $20,000 a month into their accounts but writes off most of it on their tax return, the bank statement shows the true cash flow. These programs usually average deposits over twelve or twenty-four months to create a qualifying income figure. This method aligns lending with reality rather than accounting strategy.

Other no-doc HELOCs rely primarily on assets and property value. These are often called asset-based or equity-based programs. In these loans, the lender may not even calculate income at all. They simply verify that the borrower owns the property, confirm its value, verify the existing mortgage balance, and confirm sufficient reserves. If the equity is strong enough and the borrower is not over-leveraged, the loan is approved. This is how many high-net-worth and investor clients operate. Their wealth is in assets, not pay stubs.

Interest rates on no-doc HELOCs are usually slightly higher than traditional HELOCs because the lender is taking a different type of risk. However, the trade-off is access. A slightly higher rate on money you can actually use is far better than a lower rate on money you are denied. When used properly, the return on the capital often far exceeds the extra interest cost. This is why experienced investors and business owners gladly pay for flexibility.

It is also important to understand that no-doc does not mean no verification. It means different verification. The lender still verifies the property, the equity, the borrower's identity, the credit profile, and the asset base. What they are not doing is forcing the borrower to prove income using tax documents that may not reflect their true financial strength. This creates a fairer and more efficient system for modern borrowers.

Once you understand these principles, you begin to see your home not just as a place to live, but as a financial engine. The equity in your home is a store of capital. No-doc and alternative HELOC programs are the key that unlocks that capital without forcing you into financial contortions just to satisfy outdated underwriting rules. This chapter gives you the mental framework you need to approach these programs strategically rather than emotionally, setting the stage for everything else in this book.

Practical Example: *How a No-Doc HELOC Is Approved Using Real Numbers*

Let's look at a realistic homeowner named Alex. Alex owns a home worth $600,000. He owes $240,000 on his first mortgage. This means he has $360,000 in equity. To calculate this, we subtract the mortgage from the home value. $600,000 minus $240,000 equals $360,000. This is Alex's usable equity pool. Most no-doc HELOC lenders will allow total borrowing up to 70 percent of the home's value. Seventy percent of $600,000 is $420,000. This means Alex can have up to $420,000 in total loans against his home.

Since Alex already owes $240,000, we subtract that from the $420,000 limit. $420,000 minus $240,000 equals $180,000. That means Alex can qualify for a HELOC up to $180,000, even without traditional income documentation. This decision is based almost entirely on property value and equity, not on tax returns.

Now let's look at Alex's income situation. Alex is self-employed. His tax return shows only $50,000 in taxable income because he writes off business expenses. However, his bank statements show that his business deposits average $18,000 per month. Over a year, that is $216,000 in cash flow. Even though the tax return looks weak, the bank statements reveal the real financial picture. Some lenders would use this $216,000 figure to qualify him, but even if they didn't, the equity alone already supports the loan.

Next, the lender looks at reserves. Alex has $90,000 in savings and investment accounts. The HELOC payment on $180,000 at an 8 percent interest-only rate would be about $1,200 per month. To calculate this, 8 percent of $180,000 is $14,400 per year. Dividing that by 12 gives $1,200 per month. With $90,000 in reserves, Alex could make 75 months of payments even if his income went to zero. That is more than six years. From a risk perspective, this is extremely safe.

The lender now combines three powerful facts. First, Alex has 40 percent equity remaining after the HELOC. Second, he has strong cash flow based on deposits. Third, he has massive reserves compared to the payment. All three of these reduce risk. The lender does not need to see tax returns because the numbers already prove Alex's ability to repay.

So the loan is approved. Alex now has access to $180,000 in flexible capital. If he uses that money to pay off $60,000 in credit card debt at 22 percent interest, he immediately saves money. At 22 percent, $60,000 costs $13,200 per year in interest. At 8 percent on the HELOC, the same $60,000 costs only $4,800 per year. That is a savings of $8,400 annually.

If Alex invests $100,000 into a rental property that generates $1,200 per month in net cash flow, that is $14,400 per year. His interest cost on that $100,000 at 8 percent is $8,000 per year. That leaves him with $6,400 in positive cash flow after paying the HELOC interest. The equity funded the deal, and the deal now pays for itself and produces profit.

Every number in this example ties back to the same principle: equity, assets, and cash flow are what truly matter. No-doc and alternative HELOC programs simply allow lenders to evaluate those factors honestly. When you understand the math, the fear disappears. You are no longer guessing. You are simply moving capital from one place to another in a way that increases your financial power while keeping risk controlled.

Chapter 2

Understanding the Different Types of No-Doc and Alternative HELOC Programs

No-doc and alternative documentation HELOCs are not a single product. They are an entire category of lending programs designed to serve borrowers whose financial lives do not fit into traditional tax-return underwriting. Understanding the differences between these programs is critical because each one solves a different problem. Some borrowers have strong cash flow but aggressive tax write-offs. Others have massive assets but irregular income. Some are real estate investors whose income flows through properties instead of paychecks. The power of alternative HELOC lending is that there is almost always a program that matches the borrower's true financial profile.

One of the most common types of alternative HELOC is the bank statement HELOC. Instead of using tax returns, the lender analyzes twelve or twenty-four months of personal or business bank statements. They total the deposits and average them to calculate monthly income. If a borrower deposits $15,000 per month on average, the lender may use a percentage of that as qualifying income, often between 50 and

80 percent depending on the program. This method recognizes the real money coming in rather than what remains after deductions. For business owners, this can increase qualifying income by two or three times compared to tax returns.

Another major category is asset-based HELOCs. These programs focus primarily on what the borrower owns rather than what they earn. The lender verifies the home's value, the existing mortgage balance, and the borrower's liquid assets. If the equity and reserves are strong enough, income may not even be calculated. This is extremely popular with retirees, investors, and high-net-worth borrowers who may have large portfolios but little taxable income. In these loans, the risk is controlled by keeping the loan-to-value ratio low and requiring sufficient cash or investment reserves.

There are also DSCR-style HELOCs, which are commonly used by real estate investors. DSCR stands for debt service coverage ratio. Instead of looking at the borrower's personal income, the lender looks at whether the property's rental income can support the payment. If the rent covers the HELOC payment with a safety margin, the loan is approved. This allows investors to pull equity out of rental properties without needing personal income at all. It turns the property itself into the qualifying factor. Stated income HELOCs are another option. In these programs, the borrower states their income without providing full documentation. The lender does not verify it with tax returns but still requires strong credit, equity, and reserves. These programs are designed for borrowers who have complex income streams that are difficult to document but who have strong overall financial profiles. While these programs are more restrictive than asset-based loans, they still offer far more flexibility than traditional HELOCs.

Some programs combine multiple methods. A lender may use bank statements to establish cash flow, assets to verify reserves, and equity to control risk. This layered approach allows the lender to approve borrowers who would otherwise be impossible to qualify under standard guidelines. The key is that no single metric controls the decision. Instead, the entire financial picture is evaluated.

Understanding these structures changes how you approach your own financial profile. Instead of asking, "What will a bank think of my tax return?" you begin asking, "Which program best matches how I actually earn and store money?" This shift gives you leverage. It allows you to position yourself for approval instead of hoping for it.

These programs also explain why working with a licensed mortgage broker is so important. Retail banks typically offer only one or two HELOC options. Brokers have access to dozens of lenders, each with different underwriting rules. One lender may deny you while another approves you easily using a different method. The borrower who understands the types of programs available can be matched to the right lender instead of being rejected by the wrong one.

When you understand that no-doc and alternative HELOCs are not risky loopholes but well-structured financial tools, your entire view of borrowing changes. These programs exist because modern financial lives are complex, and lending has evolved to meet that reality. The more you understand how these programs work, the more confidently you can use your home equity as a strategic financial resource.

Practical Example: *Comparing Different No-Doc HELOC Programs Using Real Numbers*

Let's look at a homeowner named Maria. Maria owns a home worth $500,000. Her current mortgage balance is $200,000. That means she has $300,000 in equity. Most alternative HELOC lenders allow up to 70 percent loan-to-value. Seventy percent of $500,000 is $350,000. Subtracting the $200,000 mortgage leaves $150,000 available for a HELOC.

Maria runs an online business. Her tax return shows only $60,000 in income, but her bank statements show she deposits $14,000 per month. Over a year, that is $168,000. A bank statement HELOC might use 70 percent of that, which equals $117,600 in qualifying income. Dividing that by 12 gives $9,800 per month. This income easily supports a $150,000 HELOC payment of about $1,000 per month at an 8 percent interest rate.

If Maria applied for a traditional HELOC, her $60,000 income might only qualify her for a much smaller line. But the bank statement program allows her to access the full $150,000 because it reflects her true cash flow.

Now consider the same Maria under an asset-based HELOC. Maria has $120,000 in savings and investment accounts. The lender calculates that her HELOC payment on $150,000 at 8 percent would be $12,000 per year, or $1,000 per month. With $120,000 in reserves, Maria has ten years of payments available even if her income stopped. From a risk standpoint, this is extremely safe. The lender may not even need to analyze her income at all.

Now imagine Maria is an investor and rents the home for $3,200 per month. A DSCR-style HELOC looks only at whether the rent covers the payment. If the HELOC payment is $1,000 and the rent is $3,200, the ratio is 3.2. That means the rent covers the payment more than three times over. That is far above the minimum requirement, so the loan is approved even if Maria's personal income is ignored.

In each case, the math leads to the same result. The $150,000 HELOC is approved, but for different reasons. In the bank statement program, cash flow supports it. In the asset-based program, reserves support it. In the DSCR program, rent supports it. The tax return becomes irrelevant.

This is why understanding the types of alternative HELOC programs is so powerful. You are no longer trapped by a single financial narrative. You are simply matching your real numbers to the right lending model. When you do that, your home equity becomes a flexible financial tool instead of a locked-up asset.

Chapter 3

How Lenders Calculate Risk Without Using Income

In traditional lending, income is treated as the primary measure of safety. If a borrower earns enough on paper to cover the payment, the loan is approved. But in no-doc and alternative HELOC programs, lenders use a completely different risk model. They understand that income can be manipulated, reduced through tax strategy, or fluctuate wildly for business owners and investors. What does not fluctuate as easily is equity, asset value, and liquidity. These are the real anchors of financial stability, and they form the backbone of alternative HELOC underwriting.

The first and most powerful risk control is loan-to-value, or LTV. LTV tells the lender how much of the home's value is being borrowed. If a borrower has a home worth $700,000 and total loans of $350,000, the LTV is 50 percent. That means half the home is owned outright with no debt against it. Even if the market drops, there is still a massive equity cushion protecting the lender. This is why no-doc HELOCs usually cap LTV around 60 to 70 percent. The lender is not betting on your income. They are betting on the value of your property and the equity buffer. The second major risk factor is liquidity. Liquidity means how much money you have that can be accessed quickly. This includes checking and savings accounts, brokerage accounts, money market funds, and even certain retirement accounts. Lenders look at liquidity to answer one simple question: if something goes wrong, can the borrower keep paying? A borrower with $150,000 in liquid assets is far less risky than someone living paycheck to paycheck, even if both show the same income. In many no-doc HELOC programs, lenders require six to twelve months of payments in reserves. This alone dramatically reduces default risk.

The third factor is credit profile. Even though income may not be verified, credit history still matters. A borrower who has consistently paid their obligations on time for years has demonstrated financial responsibility. A strong credit score tells the lender that the borrower knows how to manage debt. This is especially important in no-doc lending because it replaces the comfort that traditional income verification provides. High credit scores allow lenders to feel confident that the borrower will treat the HELOC responsibly.

Property type and location also play a major role. A single-family home in a strong housing market is far less risky than a unique or hard-to-sell property. Lenders prefer properties that can be easily sold if necessary. This is why many no-doc HELOCs are offered primarily on primary residences, second homes, or high-demand rental properties. The easier the property is to liquidate, the more flexible the lender can be.

Another key factor is payment structure. Many alternative HELOCs are interest-only during the draw period. This keeps payments low and manageable. For example, borrowing $200,000 at 8 percent interest costs $16,000 per year, or about $1,333 per month. That is much easier to support than a fully amortized loan. Lower payments reduce default risk and make it easier for the borrower to keep the line open long-term.

All of these factors combine into a holistic risk profile. Instead of asking whether your income fits into a formula, the lender asks whether your overall financial position makes default unlikely. This approach is actually more conservative in many ways than traditional lending. A borrower with strong equity, high reserves, and a solid credit history is statistically far safer than a borrower who barely qualifies based on income alone.

Once you understand how lenders think, you can begin to position yourself strategically. You realize that building equity, maintaining liquidity, and protecting your credit score are just as important as earning income. In many cases, they are more important. This is why some of the wealthiest borrowers qualify easily for no-doc HELOCs even when their tax returns show very little income. Their balance sheets tell the real story.

This chapter gives you the lens lenders use when income is removed from the equation. It is not a mystery. It is simply math and risk management. When you understand that, you stop fearing alternative lending and start using it as a tool to unlock the financial power of your home.

Practical Example: *How a No-Doc HELOC Is Approved Using Risk Math*

Let's look at a homeowner named Daniel. Daniel owns a home worth $800,000. He owes $300,000 on his first mortgage. To calculate his equity, we subtract $300,000 from $800,000, which equals $500,000. This is Daniel's equity. Most no-doc HELOC lenders allow up to 65 percent loan-to-value. Sixty-five percent of $800,000 is $520,000. That means Daniel can have up to $520,000 in total loans on his home.

Since he already owes $300,000, we subtract that from $520,000. $520,000 minus $300,000 equals $220,000. That means Daniel can qualify for a HELOC of up to $220,000 based purely on equity.

Now the lender looks at liquidity. Daniel has $160,000 in cash and investment accounts. If he draws the full $220,000

HELOC at 8 percent interest, his annual interest cost would be $17,600. Dividing by 12 gives a monthly payment of about $1,467. With $160,000 in reserves, Daniel could make about 109 months of payments, which is over nine years, even if his income went to zero. From a risk standpoint, this is extremely safe.

Next, the lender looks at Daniel's credit. His credit score is 760, and he has no late payments in the last five years. This tells the lender that Daniel has a long history of honoring his obligations. This further reduces risk.

Now look at the equity cushion. After Daniel takes the $220,000 HELOC, his total loans will be $520,000 on a home worth $800,000. That means he still has $280,000 in equity. Even if home prices dropped by 20 percent, the home would still be worth $640,000, which is more than the $520,000 owed. The lender is protected even in a major market downturn.

All of these numbers tell the same story. Daniel is a low-risk borrower. The lender does not need to see his tax returns because the equity, reserves, and credit already prove that the loan is safe.

If Daniel uses $150,000 of the HELOC to buy a rental property that produces $1,800 per month in net income, that is $21,600 per year. The interest cost on $150,000 at 8 percent is $12,000 per year. That leaves Daniel with $9,600 in positive cash flow after paying interest. The HELOC funded an income-producing asset that more than covers its own cost. Every number in this example adds up to the same conclusion. Risk is controlled not by income, but by equity, liquidity, and smart leverage. When you understand how lenders do this math, you stop seeing no-doc HELOCs as risky and start seeing them as one of the most powerful financial tools available to modern homeowners.

Chapter 4

How to Prepare Your Financial Profile for No-Doc HELOC Approval

Qualifying for a no-doc or alternative HELOC is not about luck. It is about positioning. When income is not the centerpiece of underwriting, everything else on your financial profile becomes more important. Equity, liquidity, credit, and property quality all work together to determine whether you are approved, how much you can borrow, and what rate you receive. This means that borrowers who understand how lenders think can actively shape their approval outcome long before they ever submit an application.

The first step is understanding your true equity position. Many homeowners think they know how much equity they have, but they are often wrong because they rely on outdated estimates or online tools that lag behind the real market. Lenders will use professional valuations, so you should assume that your home's value is based on what it could sell for today, not what you paid for it. If you purchased a home for $400,000 and it is now worth $600,000, that $200,000 increase is real leverage. Knowing your realistic market value allows you to calculate your true loan-to-value ratio and understand how much capital you can access.

The second step is cleaning and strengthening your credit profile. Even in no-doc lending, credit is a powerful signal of responsibility. You do not need perfect credit, but you do need to avoid recent late payments, charge-offs, or collections. Paying down revolving balances below 30 percent of their limits can dramatically increase your score. Removing small derogatory items can also have an outsized impact. Since interest rates and approval limits are tied to credit tiers, every point you improve directly translates into cheaper money and more access to equity.

The third step is increasing liquidity. Since lenders rely on reserves instead of income, having more cash or liquid investments dramatically improves your approval profile. This does not mean you need to hoard cash forever. It means that in the months leading up to your HELOC application, you want your bank and investment accounts to look strong. Selling unused assets, delaying large purchases, or temporarily holding more cash can push you into a better risk category and unlock higher borrowing limits.

The fourth step is managing your existing debt. Even though income is not verified, lenders still look at how much you already owe. If you have large balances on credit cards, personal loans, or other lines of credit, those increase your overall risk. Using cash or smaller loans to reduce high-interest debt before applying for a HELOC often increases approval odds and lowers rates. This is especially important because lenders do not want to see borrowers who are already overextended.

The fifth step is presenting the property correctly. A clean title, up-to-date insurance, and a well-maintained home all matter. Properties with unresolved liens, legal issues, or deferred maintenance raise red flags. Even though the HELOC is based on equity, the lender still wants to know that the collateral is solid and marketable. Simple things like fixing obvious damage or ensuring insurance coverage is current can make the difference between approval and denial.

Finally, documentation still matters, just not in the way most borrowers expect. You will need to provide proof of identity, ownership, mortgage statements, and asset statements. Being organized and responsive makes you look like a low-risk borrower. Lenders favor borrowers who appear financially disciplined, even when income is not part of the equation.

Preparing for a no-doc HELOC is about turning your financial life into a clean, strong, low-risk profile. When you do that, lenders compete for your business instead of rejecting you. This chapter gives you the roadmap to move from uncertainty to control.

Practical Example: *How Preparation Increases HELOC Approval Power*

Let's look at a homeowner named Sophia. Sophia owns a home currently worth $700,000. She owes $350,000 on her mortgage. That means her equity is $350,000. Most no-doc HELOC lenders allow up to 65 percent loan-to-value. Sixty-five percent of $700,000 is $455,000. Subtracting the $350,000 mortgage leaves $105,000 available for a HELOC.

At first glance, Sophia can borrow about $105,000. But her financial profile can be improved. Sophia has $40,000 in credit card balances across several cards. Those cards have total limits of $100,000, meaning she is using 40 percent of her available credit. By paying those balances down to $10,000, she reduces utilization to 10 percent. This raises her credit score by about 40 points.

With the higher credit score, a lender is willing to go to 70 percent loan-to-value instead of 65 percent. Seventy percent of $700,000 is $490,000. Subtracting the $350,000 mortgage now leaves $140,000 available instead of $105,000. That $30,000 credit card payoff just unlocked an additional $35,000 in HELOC capacity.

Now look at liquidity. Sophia had $30,000 in savings before paying down the cards. After paying $30,000 to reduce debt, she has $0 in cash. That hurts her reserve profile. Instead, she sells an unused vehicle for $50,000 and deposits it into her savings. Now she has $50,000 in reserves.

If Sophia draws the full $140,000 HELOC at 8 percent, the annual interest is $11,200. Dividing by 12 gives about $933 per month. With $50,000 in reserves, she can cover about 54 months of payments, which is four and a half years. That makes her look very safe to a lender.

By managing debt, improving credit, and increasing liquidity, Sophia transformed her profile. She started with a $105,000 HELOC limit and a weak reserve position. She ended with a $140,000 HELOC limit, strong reserves, and better pricing. The math shows how preparation directly converts into more borrowing power and lower risk.

Chapter 5

How to Use No-Doc HELOC Funds Strategically After Approval

Getting approved for a no-doc or alternative HELOC is only the beginning. What truly determines whether this tool improves or damages your financial life is how you deploy the capital after the line is open. A HELOC is not income. It is borrowed money secured by your home. When used recklessly, it can increase stress and risk. When used strategically, it can multiply your wealth, stabilize your cash flow, and dramatically reduce the cost of your debt. This chapter is about learning to think like a capital manager rather than a borrower

The first principle of using HELOC funds wisely is to understand the cost of money. Every dollar you draw from a HELOC has an interest cost. If your HELOC rate is 8 percent, then $100,000 costs $8,000 per year in interest. That is your hurdle rate. Any use of the money should either save more than that in expenses or generate more than that in returns. If you use HELOC funds to pay off credit card debt at 22 percent interest, you immediately create a positive spread. If you use it to invest in something that earns 12 percent, you also create a positive spread. If you use it to buy things that do not produce returns, you create negative leverage.

The second principle is cash flow management. Most no-doc HELOCs are interest-only during the draw period. This means your payment is based only on how much you have drawn, not on the full credit limit. You should always think in terms of monthly cash flow. If you draw $120,000 at 8 percent, your monthly cost is about $800. If the use of that $120,000 reduces your monthly expenses by $1,500 or generates $1,500 in income, you are net positive even before considering long-term benefits.

The third principle is risk separation. You never want to use HELOC funds in a way that ties your home to a single risky bet. Instead, think in terms of diversification. You might use part of the line to eliminate high-interest debt, part to fund an investment, and part to hold as liquidity. This spreads risk and protects your home from being exposed to any one failure.

The fourth principle is liquidity preservation. Even after you draw from a HELOC, you should maintain cash reserves. This ensures that you can always make payments even if an investment takes time to produce returns. This is what separates professional capital management from emotional borrowing. Liquidity is what keeps leverage safe.

The fifth principle is compounding. When you use a HELOC to replace expensive debt or fund cash-flowing assets, the savings and income can be used to either pay down the HELOC or invest further. Over time, this creates a compounding effect where your equity produces more equity. This is how smart homeowners turn a line of credit into a long-term wealth engine.

The goal of a no-doc HELOC is not to spend more. It is to move money from low-productivity uses into high-productivity uses. When you think this way, your home becomes a financial hub rather than just a place to live.

Practical Example: *Turning a HELOC Into Cash Flow and Savings*

Let's look at a homeowner named Marcus. Marcus is approved for a $200,000 no-doc HELOC at 8 percent interest. He decides to draw $150,000. The annual interest cost on $150,000 at 8 percent is $12,000. Dividing by 12 gives a monthly payment of $1,000.

Marcus has $80,000 in credit card and personal loan debt at an average interest rate of 20 percent. At 20 percent, $80,000 costs $16,000 per year in interest, or about $1,333 per month. Marcus uses $80,000 of his HELOC to pay off this debt. Now that $80,000 is costing him 8 percent instead of 20 percent.

The interest cost drops from $16,000 to $6,400 per year. That is a savings of $9,600 annually, or $800 per month.

Marcus now has $70,000 left from his HELOC draw. He uses that $70,000 as a down payment on a rental property. The rental produces $1,400 per month in net income after all expenses. The interest cost on $70,000 at 8 percent is $5,600 per year, or about $467 per month.

Now let's add everything up. Marcus's total HELOC draw is $150,000. The total monthly interest is $1,000. His debt payoff saved him $800 per month. His rental income produces $1,400 per month. Subtract the $467 HELOC interest associated with the rental portion. That leaves $933 in net rental cash flow.

Combine the savings and income. $800 from lower interest plus $933 from rental cash flow equals $1,733 per month. Subtract the full $1,000 HELOC payment and Marcus is left with $733 in positive cash flow. He is paying the HELOC, eliminating expensive debt, and earning extra income at the same time.

Every dollar of this math comes from the same principle. The HELOC moved money from high-cost debt and idle equity into lower-cost capital and productive assets. Marcus did not take on more risk. He rearranged existing risk into a structure that produces cash flow instead of draining it. This is how no-doc HELOCs become tools for financial growth instead of financial stress.

Chapter 6

Long-Term Management, Exit Strategies, and Protecting Your Home

A no-doc HELOC is not something you "set and forget." It is a living financial instrument that must be managed over time. The same flexibility that makes it powerful also makes it dangerous if left unmanaged. The goal is not just to access your equity, but to keep control of it, grow it, and eventually restore or increase the value of your home free of unnecessary risk. This chapter focuses on how to think about a HELOC over years, not months.

The first concept is draw management. Just because you have a large line of credit does not mean you should use all of it. Professional borrowers think in terms of deployment, not limits. They draw money when there is a clear purpose and a clear return or savings. They avoid emotionally driven spending. Every dollar drawn should have a role, whether that is reducing interest, producing income, or building liquidity. This keeps the HELOC working for you instead of against you.

The second concept is amortization control. Many HELOCs are interest-only during the draw period, but eventually convert to repayment. If you only ever pay interest, the balance never goes down. This is not inherently bad if the funds were used productively, but over time you should create a plan to reduce or eliminate the balance. This can be done by reinvesting profits, refinancing investments, or redirecting cash flow toward principal. The goal is to use leverage temporarily, not permanently.

The third concept is interest rate awareness. Most HELOCs have variable rates. This means your cost of borrowing can increase if market rates rise. Smart borrowers prepare for this by keeping reserves, maintaining positive cash flow from HELOC-funded assets, and avoiding over-leveraging. If rates rise, you want the ability to either absorb the increase or pay down the balance quickly.

The fourth concept is equity protection. Your home is the collateral. That means it should never be exposed to unnecessary risk. This is why diversification is critical. You should not put all HELOC funds into one investment, one business, or one idea. Spreading capital across multiple uses protects you from any single failure putting your home at risk.

The fifth concept is exit planning. Every use of a HELOC should have an exit. That exit might be selling an investment, refinancing a property, receiving business profits, or using long-term cash flow to pay down the line. When you enter a

HELOC-funded strategy, you should already know how you plan to get out. This removes stress and prevents emotional decisions.

The final concept is upgrading your financial position. The ultimate goal is not just to borrow against your home, but to increase your net worth. If your HELOC-funded investments increase your income and assets, your home equity will likely grow over time as well. Eventually, you may be able to pay off the HELOC entirely while keeping the assets it helped you acquire. That is true financial leverage done correctly.

Practical Example: *Managing a HELOC Over Five Years*

Let's look at a homeowner named Daniel who opens a $250,000 no-doc HELOC at 8 percent interest. He initially draws $200,000. The annual interest on $200,000 at 8 percent is $16,000, which equals $1,333 per month.

Daniel uses $120,000 to buy two rental properties. Each property produces $900 per month in net income, for a total of $1,800 per month. He uses the remaining $80,000 to pay off high-interest credit cards that were costing him $1,600 per month. After moving that debt to the HELOC, the interest on that $80,000 at 8 percent is about $533 per month.

Now let's calculate the monthly picture. The rental income is $1,800. The debt savings are $1,600. The HELOC interest on the full $200,000 is $1,333. Daniel's net monthly cash flow is $1,800 plus $1,600 minus $1,333, which equals $2,067. He is now cash-flow positive even while carrying the HELOC.

Daniel decides to apply $1,000 of that cash flow toward paying down the HELOC principal each month. Over one year, that is $12,000. Over five years, that is $60,000. That means after five years, his HELOC balance drops from $200,000 to $140,000.

Meanwhile, his rental properties have appreciated. Suppose each property was purchased for $150,000 and appreciates at 4 percent per year. After five years, each property is worth about $182,000. Together, they are worth $364,000, up from $300,000. That is a $64,000 increase in asset value.

Now Daniel has a HELOC balance of $140,000, rental properties worth $364,000, and continuing rental income of $1,800 per month. He could sell one property and pay off most of the HELOC, or refinance the rentals and pay it off entirely.

Every number in this example shows how strategic use, cash flow, and disciplined repayment turn a HELOC into a wealth-building engine rather than a long-term liability.

Chapter 7

Common Mistakes, Warning Signs, and How to Avoid Financial Traps

No-doc and alternative HELOC programs are powerful, but power without discipline can become dangerous. Most financial damage does not come from the tool itself, but from how people misuse it. This chapter is designed to protect you from the most common mistakes that cause homeowners to lose control of their equity, overextend themselves, or turn a smart financial move into long-term stress. Understanding these risks allows you to use leverage with confidence instead of fear.

The first major mistake is treating a HELOC like income. When the money hits your account, it feels like cash you earned. In reality, it is borrowed money secured by your home. If you spend it on lifestyle upgrades, vacations, or non-productive purchases, you create permanent debt with no way to repay it except future income. Smart borrowers only use HELOC funds to reduce costs, increase income, or create long-term value. If a purchase does not improve your financial position, it does not belong on a HELOC.

The second mistake is over-leveraging. Just because a lender approves you for a large line does not mean you should use all of it. Equity is a safety buffer. When you draw too much, you remove that buffer. If property values fall or interest rates rise, you can become trapped. Professional borrowers always leave unused equity as protection against market changes and emergencies.

The third mistake is ignoring interest rate risk. Most HELOCs are variable rate. That means your payment can increase. Borrowers who calculate their strategy based on today's low payment without planning for higher rates are gambling with their home. You should always assume rates will go up and ensure your cash flow and reserves can handle it.

The fourth mistake is failing to maintain liquidity. Even when investments are performing well, unexpected expenses happen. Medical issues, market downturns, or tenant vacancies can disrupt cash flow. If you have no cash reserves, you are forced to make desperate decisions. Liquidity is what turns leverage from risky to safe.

The fifth mistake is emotional investing. HELOC money feels easier to spend because it is not tied to your paycheck. This makes people more likely to take speculative risks, chase trends, or invest in things they do not fully understand. Every use of HELOC funds should be based on math, not excitement. The final mistake is having no exit plan. Every HELOC-funded move should have a clear path to repayment. Whether it is refinancing, selling an asset, or using cash flow, you should know how the balance will eventually be reduced. Borrowers who skip this step often end up trapped in long-term debt.

By recognizing these traps, you protect not just your finances, but your home. The goal of leverage is to increase your freedom, not to risk the roof over your head.

Practical Example: *How a Bad HELOC Strategy Turns Into a Trap*

Let's look at a homeowner named Ryan. Ryan is approved for a $250,000 no-doc HELOC at 8 percent interest. He immediately draws the full amount. The annual interest on $250,000 at 8 percent is $20,000, which equals about $1,667 per month.

Ryan uses $100,000 to buy a luxury car, $50,000 on home upgrades, and $100,000 on speculative investments. None of these produce income. Now Ryan has no extra cash flow to pay the HELOC. He must rely entirely on his regular income.

After one year, interest rates rise from 8 percent to 10 percent. Now the annual interest on $250,000 is $25,000, or about $2,083 per month. Ryan's payment increases by $416 per month. Ryan also has only $10,000 in savings. That covers less than five months of payments. If Ryan loses income or faces an emergency, he is at risk of default.

Now compare this to a smarter version of Ryan. Instead of drawing the full $250,000, he draws only $150,000. The interest at 8 percent is $12,000 per year, or $1,000 per month. He uses $80,000 to pay off high-interest debt that was costing him $1,600 per month. He uses $50,000 to buy an investment that produces $900 per month. He keeps $20,000 in cash.

Now let's do the math. Ryan saves $1,600 per month from debt payoff. He earns $900 per month from his investment. That is $2,500 per month. Subtract the $1,000 HELOC payment and Ryan is left with $1,500 in positive cash flow. If rates rise to 10 percent, his payment becomes $1,250. He still has $1,250 in positive cash flow.

This simple math shows how the same HELOC can either become a trap or a tool. The difference is discipline, planning, and understanding how every number affects your long-term security.

Chapter 8

Scaling Wealth With No-Doc HELOCs and Strategic Leverage

Once you understand how to safely access and manage a no-doc HELOC, the next step is learning how to scale. Scaling does not mean taking reckless risks or maxing out your line. It means using leverage in a controlled, repeatable way that steadily increases your net worth, income, and financial resilience. Wealthy families have used this strategy for generations by borrowing against appreciating assets to acquire more assets. A no-doc HELOC simply allows modern homeowners to do the same.

The first principle of scaling is using equity as a renewable resource. When you use your HELOC to acquire income-producing assets, those assets generate cash flow and appreciation. That appreciation increases your overall net worth, which in turn creates more borrowing capacity in the future. This creates a cycle where equity leads to assets, assets lead to income, and income leads to more equity. The key is that the cycle must be positive at every step.

The second principle is capital recycling. Instead of letting money sit idle after an investment stabilizes, you can refinance, sell, or reposition it to repay your HELOC and free up the line again. This allows you to reuse the same equity multiple times without permanently increasing risk. Professional investors call this velocity of capital. The faster you can safely recycle capital, the faster you can grow.

The third principle is risk layering. When scaling, you do not put all your equity into one deal. You spread it across multiple assets with different risk profiles. Some investments may be stable and low-return, like rental properties. Others may be higher growth, like businesses. The combination smooths volatility and protects your home.

The fourth principle is cash flow dominance. Every stage of scaling should improve your monthly cash flow. If your leverage strategy makes you more fragile month to month, it is not sustainable. Positive cash flow gives you the ability to absorb rate increases, vacancies, and market cycles without panic.

The fifth principle is balance sheet growth. The real goal is not just income, but net worth. If your HELOC-funded assets grow faster than the HELOC balance, your financial position improves even if the debt remains. This is why strategic leverage works.

When used correctly, a no-doc HELOC becomes a private banking system. Your home provides capital. Your investments provide income. Your discipline provides safety. Together, they create a scalable wealth engine.

Practical Example: *Scaling a Portfolio Using One HELOC*

Let's look at a homeowner named Laura. Laura opens a $300,000 no-doc HELOC at 8 percent interest. She initially draws $200,000. The interest cost is $16,000 per year, or about $1,333 per month.

Laura uses $150,000 to buy two rental properties. Each property produces $1,100 per month in net income, for a total of $2,200. She uses the remaining $50,000 to invest in a small business that produces $600 per month in profit.

Now let's calculate the cash flow. Laura's total income from HELOC-funded assets is $2,200 plus $600, which equals $2,800 per month. Her HELOC interest cost is $1,333. That leaves $1,467 in positive cash flow.

Laura decides to use $1,000 of that cash flow to pay down the HELOC principal each month. After one year, she has paid $12,000. After three years, she has paid $36,000. Her HELOC balance drops from $200,000 to $164,000.

Meanwhile, her rental properties were purchased for $300,000 total. After three years of 4 percent appreciation, they are worth about $337,000. That is $37,000 in appreciation.

Now Laura's total asset value is $337,000 plus her business investment, while her HELOC balance is only $164,000. Her equity position has grown, even though she used leverage.

Laura can now refinance the rentals or open a second HELOC to access new capital while keeping her original line under control. This is how one HELOC becomes a multi-asset portfolio.

Every number in this example shows how leverage, when combined with cash flow and appreciation, compounds over time instead of creating stress.

Chapter 9

HELOC Risk Management, Market Cycles, and Staying Protected

Using a no-doc or alternative HELOC is not about blind optimism. It is about understanding risk better than the average borrower. Every market goes through cycles. Interest rates rise and fall. Property values move up and down. Income changes. The borrowers who succeed long-term are not the ones who avoid risk entirely, but the ones who build systems that survive volatility. This chapter teaches you how to structure your HELOC strategy so it works in good markets and bad.

The first layer of risk management is equity preservation. Your home is the foundation of the entire strategy. That means you must always leave a margin of safety. If lenders allow 70 percent loan-to-value, that does not mean you should operate at 70 percent. Smart borrowers aim for 50 to 60 percent whenever possible. This protects you from market declines. If home prices drop 15 or 20 percent, you still have plenty of equity and no refinancing pressure.

The second layer is payment resilience. HELOCs are variable-rate. That means your payment can increase. Your strategy should always assume that rates will rise. If you can afford the payment only at today's rate, you are already at risk. A safe structure is one where your cash flow from HELOC-funded uses can absorb at least a two to three percent increase in rates without stress.

The third layer is income diversification. Never rely on a single income source to support your HELOC. If you use your line to fund investments, those investments should be diversified. Rental properties, businesses, savings from debt reduction, and liquid reserves should all work together. When one slows down, the others cover the gap.

The fourth layer is liquidity buffers. Cash is what prevents forced selling. You should always maintain enough liquid reserves to cover at least six to twelve months of HELOC payments. This gives you time to react to changes instead of being forced into bad decisions.

The fifth layer is ongoing monitoring. A HELOC strategy should be reviewed at least twice a year. Check your balances, interest rates, asset values, and cash flow. Adjust if necessary. Risk management is not something you do once. It is something you maintain.

The final layer is exit readiness. You should always know how you would reduce or eliminate your HELOC balance if needed.

That could be selling an asset, refinancing, or redirecting cash flow. Having a plan removes panic from the equation.

When these layers work together, your HELOC becomes resilient. It is no longer fragile or dependent on perfect conditions. It becomes a financial system that can handle change.

Practical Example: *Stress-Testing a HELOC Strategy*

Let's look at a homeowner named Kevin. Kevin opens a $250,000 no-doc HELOC at 7.5 percent interest. He draws $180,000. His annual interest cost is $13,500, which is $1,125 per month.

Kevin uses $120,000 to buy two rental properties that produce $1,700 per month in total net income. He uses $40,000 to pay off high-interest debt that was costing him $900 per month. He keeps $20,000 in savings.

Now let's calculate his baseline cash flow. Rental income is $1,700. Debt savings are $900. Total benefit is $2,600. Subtract the HELOC interest of $1,125 and Kevin has $1,475 in positive cash flow.

Now let's stress-test. Interest rates rise from 7.5 percent to 10 percent. The annual interest on $180,000 becomes $18,000, which is $1,500 per month. Kevin's payment increases by $375.

His rental income stays $1,700. His debt savings remain $900. Total is still $2,600. Subtract the new HELOC payment of $1,500 and Kevin is left with $1,100 in positive cash flow. He is still safe even after a big rate increase.

Now imagine one rental is vacant and income drops by $850. Kevin's rental income becomes $850 instead of $1,700. His debt savings are still $900. Total cash flow is $1,750. Subtract the $1,500 HELOC payment and he has $250 left. He is still positive.

Kevin also has $20,000 in savings. At a $1,500 payment, that covers over 13 months. That gives him time to fix vacancies or refinance if needed.

Every number shows how layered risk management keeps Kevin safe even when multiple things go wrong. This is how HELOC leverage is turned into a controlled, professional financial system instead of a gamble.

Chapter 10

The Smart Borrower's Home Equity Blueprint

This chapter brings everything together. By now, you understand how no-doc and alternative HELOCs work, how lenders evaluate risk, how to prepare your profile, how to deploy funds, how to scale, and how to manage risk over time. What remains is to turn all of this into a repeatable blueprint you can use for the rest of your financial life. Wealth is not built through one transaction. It is built through systems that are applied consistently, year after year.

The first step in the blueprint is to always start with equity mapping. You should know the current market value of your home, the balance of your mortgage, and your true available equity. This gives you a financial dashboard. Every six to twelve months, you update this information. As your home appreciates and your mortgage balance decreases, your borrowing power grows. This is the foundation of your private banking system.

The second step is financial positioning. Before using a HELOC, you optimize credit, reduce high-interest debt, and strengthen liquidity. This ensures that when you access equity, you get the best rates and the highest limits. This step also ensures you are entering leverage from a position of strength rather than desperation.

The third step is strategic deployment. Every dollar drawn must have a purpose. That purpose must either save more interest than it costs, produce more income than it costs, or build long-term asset value. If it does none of these, it does not belong in the strategy. This keeps your leverage productive instead of destructive.

The fourth step is cash flow dominance. Your HELOC strategy must improve your monthly financial position. If your cash flow gets tighter after using your HELOC, something is wrong. Positive cash flow is what allows you to survive market changes and stay in control.

The fifth step is capital recycling. As investments mature, you refinance, sell, or reposition them to pay down the HELOC and free up your line again. This allows the same equity to be used repeatedly to build a portfolio over time.

The final step is risk control. You always maintain reserves, diversify uses, and monitor your financial position. This ensures your home remains protected while your wealth grows. When these steps are followed, your home is no longer just a place to live. It becomes the engine of a long-term wealth system that you control.

Practical Example: *A Five-Year Home Equity Wealth Plan*

Let's look at a homeowner named Olivia. Olivia owns a home worth $750,000 and owes $350,000 on her mortgage. That means she has $400,000 in equity. A no-doc HELOC at 70 percent LTV allows total borrowing up to $525,000. Subtracting the $350,000 mortgage leaves $175,000 available.

Olivia opens a $175,000 HELOC at 8 percent interest. She initially draws $150,000. The annual interest is $12,000, or $1,000 per month.

She uses $90,000 to pay off credit cards and personal loans that were costing her $1,800 per month. She uses $60,000 to buy two rental units that together produce $1,200 per month in net income.

Now let's do the math. Debt savings are $1,800 per month. Rental income is $1,200. Total benefit is $3,000. Subtract the $1,000 HELOC interest and Olivia is left with $2,000 in positive cash flow.

She uses $1,200 of that to pay down the HELOC principal. Over one year, that is $14,400. Over five years, that is $72,000. Her HELOC balance drops from $150,000 to

$78,000. Meanwhile, her rental units, purchased for $120,000 total, appreciate at 4 percent per year. After five years, they are worth about $146,000. That is $26,000 in appreciation.

Now Olivia has $146,000 in rental property value and only $78,000 left on her HELOC. She could sell the rentals, pay off the HELOC, and still have $68,000 left. Or she could refinance and keep the income.

Every number in this example shows how a disciplined HELOC blueprint turns home equity into a growing financial system instead of a one-time loan.

Chapter 11

Turning Home Equity Into a Lifetime Financial System

Most people think of home equity as something they will use once or twice in their life. They either refinance, take a HELOC, or wait until they sell the house. Wealthy families think very differently. They view home equity as part of a lifelong financial system that works alongside their income, businesses, and investments. When no-doc and alternative HELOCs are used correctly, your home becomes a private banking platform that can fund opportunity after opportunity without ever requiring you to sell or disrupt your lifestyle.

The first principle of a lifetime equity system is continuity. Instead of closing and reopening loans, you keep a HELOC active as long as possible. Even when the balance is paid down to zero, the line remains available. This means your home is always ready to provide liquidity. Emergencies, investments, and strategic moves can all be handled without scrambling for financing. This flexibility is what separates financially secure households from those that are always reacting to circumstances. The second principle is compounding through reuse. Each time you use your HELOC to fund something productive, you increase your income or assets. Those gains either create more equity or more cash flow. That new financial strength then allows you to borrow again, often at better terms, to fund the next opportunity. Over time, this creates a compounding loop. The home supports investments, investments support income, and income strengthens the home.

The third principle is generational planning. A well-managed HELOC strategy does not end with you. As your property appreciates and your debt is paid down, your equity grows. That equity can be used to fund children's education, family businesses, or long-term investments. Instead of passing down debt, you pass down a financial system that produces options and stability.

The fourth principle is tax efficiency. Borrowing against equity is often far more tax efficient than selling assets. When you sell, you may trigger capital gains taxes. When you borrow, you access capital without triggering a taxable event. This allows your assets to keep growing while you use their value. Over decades, this difference can amount to hundreds of thousands of dollars.

The fifth principle is independence. A lifetime HELOC strategy reduces your dependence on banks, employers, and even market timing. When you have access to your own capital, you are not forced to make decisions based on short-term pressures. You can wait for the right opportunities and move quickly when they appear.

The final principle is discipline. A HELOC system only works if it is managed with intention. You must track balances, protect equity, maintain liquidity, and use leverage only when it improves your position. When done properly, this turns your home into a financial anchor rather than a financial risk.

Practical Example: *Building a 20-Year Equity System*

Let's look at a homeowner named Anthony. Anthony buys a home for $500,000 with a $400,000 mortgage. Over ten years, the home appreciates to $750,000 and the mortgage is paid down to $300,000. That means Anthony has $450,000 in equity.

Anthony opens a no doc HELOC at 70 percent LTV. Seventy percent of $750,000 is $525,000. Subtracting the $300,000 mortgage leaves $225,000 available.

Anthony draws $150,000 to start a small rental portfolio. The interest on $150,000 at 8 percent is $12,000 per year, or $1,000 per month. The rentals produce $1,800 per month in net income. Anthony uses $800 of that income to pay down the HELOC principal. Over one year, that is $9,600. Over ten years, that is $96,000. His HELOC balance drops to $54,000.

Meanwhile, the rental properties, purchased for $150,000, appreciate at 4 percent per year. After ten years, they are worth about $222,000. That is $72,000 in appreciation.

Now Anthony has rental properties worth $222,000 and a HELOC balance of only $54,000. He can sell one property, pay off the HELOC, and still have significant equity left. Or he can refinance the rentals and continue the cycle.

Anthony's home continues to appreciate. Suppose after 20 years it is worth $1,000,000 and the mortgage is nearly paid off. He now has hundreds of thousands of dollars in equity and a portfolio of income-producing assets that were all funded by his original HELOC.

Every number in this example shows how disciplined reuse of home equity turns a single house into a multi-decade wealth engine that supports not just one generation, but the next.

Chapter 12

The Future of Home Equity, Smart Borrowing, and Your Financial Advantage

Home equity is entering a new era. For decades, homeowners were limited by rigid underwriting, slow banks, and outdated income rules that did not reflect how modern people actually earn and store wealth. No-doc and alternative HELOC programs represent a structural shift in finance. They move power away from bureaucracy and toward the borrower's balance sheet. As technology, financial data, and private lending continue to evolve, the homeowners who understand this system will have a permanent advantage over those who rely only on traditional mortgages.

The first major change shaping the future is data-driven underwriting. Lenders no longer need tax returns to understand financial strength. They can see real-time bank activity, asset balances, rent flows, and property performance. This allows them to make more accurate lending decisions. For borrowers, this means that your true financial behavior matters more than how it looks on paper. Consistent deposits, strong balances, and clean credit will increasingly replace old documentation models.

The second change is the rise of asset-based lending. As more people build wealth through real estate, online businesses, investments, and decentralized income streams, lenders will continue to shift toward equity and assets as the primary form of collateral. Homes will be treated not just as shelter, but as financial hubs. HELOCs will become more flexible, faster, and more integrated into personal finance platforms.

The third change is borrower empowerment. With better access to information, homeowners are no longer dependent on a single bank's opinion. Brokers, fintech lenders, and private capital are creating competition. This competition drives better terms, better products, and better access to equity. The borrowers who understand how to position themselves will be able to negotiate from strength.

The fourth change is strategic leverage becoming mainstream. What was once reserved for real estate investors and high-net-worth families is becoming available to everyday homeowners. Using equity to fund businesses, eliminate debt, and create passive income will no longer be niche. It will become a standard financial strategy for those who want control over their money.

The final change is long-term financial independence. When you can access capital without selling assets or relying on income, you gain freedom. You can invest when others are stuck. You can handle emergencies without panic. You can grow wealth without giving it away in taxes. The future belongs to borrowers who think like capital managers, not like paycheck recipients.

This book is not about borrowing more. It is about borrowing smarter. When you use home equity with intention, discipline, and strategy, you step into a financial system that was once reserved for the wealthy. The tools now exist for you to do the same.

Practical Example: *Positioning for the Future With Home Equity*

Let's look at a homeowner named Rachel. Rachel owns a home worth $900,000 and owes $400,000 on her mortgage. That means she has $500,000 in equity. A 70 percent LTV HELOC allows total borrowing up to $630,000. Subtracting the $400,000 mortgage leaves $230,000 available.

Rachel opens a $230,000 no-doc HELOC at 8 percent interest. She initially draws $180,000. The annual interest is $14,400, or $1,200 per month.

She uses $100,000 to eliminate high-interest debt that was costing her $2,000 per month. She uses $80,000 to invest in a diversified portfolio of rental properties and businesses that produces $1,600 per month.

Now let's calculate the impact. Her debt savings are $2,000. Her investment income is $1,600. That totals $3,600 per month. Subtract the $1,200 HELOC payment and Rachel has $2,400 in positive cash flow.

Rachel uses $1,500 of that cash flow to pay down the HELOC principal. Over one year, that is $18,000. Over five years, that is $90,000. Her HELOC balance drops from $180,000 to $90,000.

Meanwhile, her investments, originally purchased for $80,000, grow at 6 percent per year. After five years, they are worth about $107,000. That is $27,000 in appreciation.

Now Rachel has investments worth $107,000 and a HELOC balance of $90,000. She could sell the investments, pay off the HELOC, and still have profit. Or she could refinance and continue scaling.

Every number shows how the future of home equity belongs to borrowers who use it as a strategic advantage rather than a last resort.

Chapter 13

Building a Zero-Stress HELOC System That Runs on Autopilot

The ultimate goal of using a no-doc or alternative HELOC is not to constantly think about it. The goal is to design a system so stable, cash-flow positive, and well-structured that it operates quietly in the background while you live your life. This chapter is about turning everything you have learned into a low-maintenance financial machine that protects your home, grows your wealth, and removes stress instead of creating it.

The first component of an autopilot HELOC system is automated cash flow control. All income generated from HELOC-funded investments should be routed through one central account. From that account, three automatic transfers should be set up. The first covers the HELOC interest payment. The second goes into a reserve account. The third goes toward principal reduction or reinvestment. This removes emotion and ensures that every dollar is assigned a job the moment it arrives.

The second component is buffer design. A HELOC system should always be designed so that the payment can be covered by at least two independent sources. For example, rental income and debt savings, or business income and investment dividends. If one stream slows down, the other covers the payment. This is what creates psychological and financial safety.

The third component is reserve layering. You should not rely on one pile of cash. You should maintain at least three layers of liquidity. The first is checking and savings for short-term needs. The second is investment accounts that can be accessed quickly. The third is unused HELOC capacity. Together, these create a deep safety net that allows you to operate with confidence.

The fourth component is annual optimization. Once per year, you should review your HELOC balance, interest rate, asset values, and cash flow. If an investment has appreciated, you may refinance it to pay down the HELOC. If your home has increased in value, you may increase your credit line. This keeps your system aligned with reality instead of drifting into inefficiency.

The fifth component is simplicity. You do not need dozens of investments or complicated structures. A few high-quality, cash-flowing uses of your HELOC are enough. Complexity increases stress. Simplicity increases control.

When these components are in place, your HELOC becomes

invisible. It quietly turns your home equity into income, growth, and security without constant management. That is the true goal of smart leverage.

Practical Example: *Designing a HELOC System That Runs Itself*

Let's look at a homeowner named Emily. Emily opens a $300,000 no-doc HELOC at 8 percent interest. She draws $200,000. The annual interest is $16,000, which is $1,333 per month.

Emily uses $140,000 to buy three rental units that produce a combined $2,100 per month in net income. She uses $60,000 to pay off high-interest debt that was costing her $1,200 per month.

Now let's calculate the cash flow. Rental income is $2,100. Debt savings are $1,200. Total benefit is $3,300. Subtract the HELOC interest of $1,333 and Emily is left with $1,967 per month.

Emily sets up three automatic transfers. $1,333 goes to the HELOC payment. $400 goes into a reserve account. $234 goes toward HELOC principal reduction. That totals $1,967.

Over one year, Emily saves $4,800 in reserves and pays $2,808 toward principal. Over five years, she saves $24,000 in reserves and pays $14,040 toward principal. Meanwhile, her rental properties appreciate. If the $140,000 in properties grows at 4 percent per year, after five years they are worth about $170,000. That is $30,000 in appreciation.

Now Emily has $24,000 in reserves, $30,000 in property appreciation, and a reduced HELOC balance. She could refinance the rentals, pay off the HELOC, and keep the system running. Every number in this example shows how automation turns leverage into a calm, predictable wealth engine instead of a source of anxiety.

Chapter 14

Using Home Equity to Achieve Total Financial Freedom

At this stage of the journey, home equity is no longer just a financial tool. It becomes the cornerstone of financial independence. When a no-doc or alternative HELOC is integrated correctly into your life, it replaces stress with optionality. Optionality means you are no longer forced to work, sell, or sacrifice just to survive. You have choices. This chapter is about using everything you have learned to reach a point where your income, assets, and equity work together to support your lifestyle permanently.

The first principle of financial freedom through equity is income replacement. The goal is not to borrow forever, but to use borrowed capital to build income streams that eventually replace your need for active work. Rental income, business profits, dividends, and interest savings all stack on top of each other. Over time, this passive and semi-passive income can equal or exceed what you earn from your job or business.

The second principle is lifestyle stability. A HELOC-based wealth system should not require you to downsize or live in fear. It should create smoother cash flow, fewer debt obligations, and larger safety cushions. When your investments and debt restructuring create more income than expenses, your financial life becomes stable even if markets fluctuate.

The third principle is inflation protection. Home equity is tied to real assets. Real estate, rents, and businesses tend to rise with inflation. When you borrow at fixed or semi-fixed rates and invest in assets that inflate, the real value of your debt shrinks over time. This is one of the most powerful wealth-building forces available to homeowners.

The fourth principle is time freedom. When your equity-powered system generates enough income, you can choose how you spend your time. You can work less, focus on family, travel, or build projects that matter to you. This is the true return on leverage.

The fifth principle is legacy creation. A well-managed HELOC system leaves behind assets, not burdens. Your children inherit income-producing property, businesses, and equity rather than debt and stress. That is generational wealth built from a single home.

Practical Example: *Reaching Financial Freedom With One HELOC*

Let's look at a homeowner named Victor. Victor owns a home worth $1,000,000 and owes $400,000 on his mortgage. That means he has $600,000 in equity. At 70 percent loan-to-value, he can have total loans of $700,000. Subtracting the $400,000 mortgage leaves $300,000 available.

Victor opens a $300,000 no-doc HELOC at 8 percent interest. He draws $250,000. The annual interest is $20,000, which is $1,667 per month.

Victor uses $180,000 to buy four rental properties that produce a combined $3,200 per month in net income. He uses $70,000 to pay off remaining personal debt that was costing him $1,500 per month.

Now let's calculate the cash flow. Rental income is $3,200. Debt savings are $1,500. Total benefit is $4,700. Subtract the HELOC payment of $1,667 and Victor is left with $3,033 per month in positive cash flow.

Victor's household living expenses are $2,500 per month. His HELOC strategy now fully covers his lifestyle with $533 left over. That extra money can be saved, invested, or used to pay down the HELOC.

Over five years, if Victor uses $1,500 per month to pay down the HELOC, that is $90,000. His HELOC balance drops from $250,000 to $160,000. Meanwhile, his rental properties, purchased for $180,000, appreciate at 4 percent per year. After five years, they are worth about $219,000.

Now Victor has $219,000 in rental assets and only $160,000 left on the HELOC. He could sell one or two rentals, pay off the HELOC, and still keep income. Every number shows how home equity, when used with discipline, can produce lasting financial freedom.

Chapter 15

Your Personalized HELOC Wealth Roadmap

Everything you have learned so far leads to one final truth: there is no single "best" way to use a no-doc or alternative HELOC. The right strategy is the one that fits your life, your income, your risk tolerance, and your long-term goals. This chapter is about turning theory into a personalized roadmap that you can follow for decades. When you customize your HELOC strategy, it stops feeling like leverage and starts feeling like a financial operating system designed specifically for you.

The first step in building your roadmap is defining your financial destination. Some people want monthly cash flow. Others want long-term net worth. Others want to eliminate debt or retire early. Your HELOC strategy should be built around that destination. If your goal is cash flow, you focus on income-producing uses. If your goal is net worth, you focus on appreciating assets. If your goal is stability, you focus on debt elimination and reserves. There is no wrong answer, but there is a wrong strategy for the wrong goal.

The second step is understanding your starting point. You should know your home value, mortgage balance, credit score, cash reserves, and existing debt. This is your financial snapshot. From this snapshot, you calculate how much equity you can access safely and how much payment you can comfortably support. This prevents overreach and ensures your plan is realistic.

The third step is sequencing. You do not do everything at once. You might start by using your HELOC to eliminate high-interest debt. Then you use the improved cash flow to invest. Then you use investment income to pay down the HELOC. This sequence keeps risk low and momentum high.

The fourth step is flexibility. Life changes. Markets change. Your roadmap should be reviewed and adjusted annually. If an opportunity appears, you may accelerate. If risk increases, you may slow down. The roadmap is a guide, not a prison.

The fifth step is accountability. Track your numbers. Watch your balances, your cash flow, and your asset values. When you see progress, you stay motivated. When you see danger, you correct course early.

A personalized HELOC roadmap is what turns financial knowledge into financial results. Without it, you are guessing. With it, you are executing a plan.

Practical Example: *Building a Custom HELOC Plan*

Let's look at a homeowner named Natalie. Natalie owns a home worth $650,000 and owes $300,000. That means she has $350,000 in equity. At 70 percent LTV, total loans can be $455,000. Subtracting the $300,000 mortgage leaves $155,000 available.

Natalie opens a $155,000 no-doc HELOC at 8 percent interest. She draws $120,000. The annual interest is $9,600, which is $800 per month.

Natalie has $50,000 in credit card and personal loan debt that costs her $1,200 per month. She uses $50,000 of the HELOC to pay it off. Now she saves $1,200 per month and pays about $333 in HELOC interest on that portion.

She uses the remaining $70,000 to invest in two rental units that produce $1,300 per month in net income. The interest cost on $70,000 at 8 percent is $467 per month.

Now let's add everything up. Debt savings are $1,200. Rental income is $1,300. Total benefit is $2,500. The total HELOC interest is $800. That leaves Natalie with $1,700 in positive cash flow.

Natalie decides to use $1,000 of that to pay down the HELOC principal. Over one year, that is $12,000. Over five years, that is $60,000. Her HELOC balance drops from $120,000 to $60,000.

Meanwhile, her rental properties, purchased for $70,000, appreciate at 4 percent per year. After five years, they are worth about $85,000.

Now Natalie has $85,000 in rental assets and only $60,000 left on her HELOC. She could sell the rentals, pay off the HELOC, and still have profit. Or she could refinance and continue growing. Every number in this example shows how a personalized roadmap turns home equity into a long-term wealth plan.

Final Thoughts

The Power You Already Own

Home equity is one of the most misunderstood and underutilized financial resources in the world. For most homeowners, it sits quietly in the background, growing with inflation and market appreciation, while their financial lives remain constrained by high-interest debt, limited cash flow, and missed opportunities. This book was written to change that. Not by encouraging reckless borrowing, but by teaching you how to think about money, risk, and assets the same way sophisticated investors and financially powerful families have done for generations. When you understand that your home is not just shelter but a balance-sheet asset, everything about your financial life begins to shift.

No-doc and alternative HELOCs are not shortcuts. They are modern financial instruments designed for a world where income is complex, businesses are digital, and wealth is often stored in assets rather than paychecks. They give you access to capital without forcing you to sell, downsize, or distort your financial reality just to satisfy outdated underwriting models. Used properly, they restore something most people lose as adults: financial flexibility. Flexibility is what allows you to handle emergencies, pursue opportunities, and design a life that is not controlled by monthly bills or employer dependence.

Throughout this book, you have seen one consistent theme repeat over and over: the difference between financial stress and financial freedom is not how much you earn, but how well you manage and deploy capital. High-income earners often stay broke because they misuse money. Modest-income households become wealthy because they use assets strategically. A no-doc HELOC gives you the same toolset that large investors and corporations use every day: the ability to borrow against assets while allowing those assets to keep growing. That is the core of modern wealth building.

What makes this approach so powerful is that it does not require you to be perfect. You do not need flawless credit, massive income, or a complex portfolio to begin. You need understanding, discipline, and a plan. By focusing on equity, liquidity, and cash flow instead of just income, you shift into a more resilient financial model. One where your home supports your goals instead of limiting them. One where debt becomes a tool instead of a burden. One where you can move forward even when traditional banks would say no.

Perhaps the most important lesson in this book is that risk is not eliminated by avoiding leverage. Risk is managed by structure. When you leave equity in your home, maintain reserves, diversify your uses, and keep positive cash flow, leverage becomes safe and predictable. It becomes something you control rather than something that controls you. This is why the same strategies that destroy unprepared borrowers quietly enrich disciplined ones. The math is not complicated. The mindset is what makes the difference.

You also learned that time is your greatest ally. A HELOC used once can change a year. A HELOC used repeatedly, recycled wisely, and paired with appreciation and cash flow can change a lifetime. Over decades, the compounding effect of even small monthly advantages becomes enormous. Interest saved, income earned, and assets accumulated all stack on top of each other. What begins as a single line of credit becomes a self-reinforcing financial system that supports you through different stages of life.

And then there is the emotional side, which is rarely discussed but deeply important. Financial stress is one of the leading causes of anxiety, relationship conflict, and poor health. A well-managed equity strategy removes much of that stress by replacing uncertainty with options. When you know you can access capital if needed, when you know your investments are covering your payments, and when you know your home is protected by equity and reserves, you experience a kind of financial calm that most people never feel. That calm is worth as much as the money itself.

This book was not written to make you reckless. It was written to make you powerful. Power in finance does not come from having no debt. It comes from having control over your debt, your assets, and your future. When you use no-doc and alternative HELOCs intelligently, you step into that control. You stop being dependent on banks, employers, or luck. You begin operating your own private financial system, using your home as the foundation.

As you move forward, remember that every financial decision should serve one purpose: increasing your freedom. Freedom to choose how you spend your time. Freedom to handle emergencies without fear. Freedom to invest when opportunities appear. Freedom to build something that lasts beyond you. Home equity, used wisely, is one of the most direct paths to that freedom.

The power is already in your hands. You have been sitting on it the entire time.

How to Get a Personalized HELOC Review

If you found *HELOC Fundamentals: How Home Equity Lines of Credit Really Work — and How to Use Them Safely* helpful, you may want to see how these concepts apply to your own home, credit profile, and financial goals.

Every homeowner's situation is unique. Home value, mortgage balance, credit history, income type, and state-specific lending rules all affect how much equity you can access, what type of HELOC you may qualify for, and what terms may be available. The examples in this book are designed to teach how HELOCs work — but your real options can only be determined by reviewing your actual numbers.

If you would like a **no-obligation Home Equity Line of Credit review**, you can request one here:

Email:info@FinibiMortgage.com

A licensed mortgage broker will review your information and explain what HELOC and home equity options may be available to you based on your specific situation.

No cost. No pressure. No obligation.

Joseph G. Correa

About the Author

Joseph G. Correa is a licensed mortgage broker and the founder of Finibi Mortgage, a Florida-based brokerage specializing in home equity, real estate investment financing, and alternative lending strategies for homeowners, business owners, and investors. With more than two decades of experience in mortgage lending, underwriting, and financial structuring, Joseph has helped thousands of borrowers access capital using intelligent, low-risk leverage rather than high-interest consumer debt.

Unlike traditional loan officers who focus only on closing transactions, Joseph's approach is rooted in long-term financial strategy. He believes that mortgages, HELOCs, and credit lines should be used as tools for building wealth, protecting cash flow, and creating financial resilience — not as traps that keep families locked into decades of unnecessary interest payments. This philosophy has made him a trusted advisor for entrepreneurs, real estate investors, and self-employed borrowers who need flexible, modern financing solutions that banks often fail to provide.

Joseph is widely known for his expertise in home equity lines of credit, no-documentation and bank-statement loan programs, investor financing, and creative equity based strategies such as debt-elimination systems and capital recycling. His ability to translate complex lending rules into simple, actionable guidance has helped homeowners turn idle equity into productive capital for investments, businesses, and passive income.

Through his education platform, Finibi Academy, Joseph has trained tens of thousands of students worldwide in credit, mortgage strategy, real estate financing, and financial independence. His courses and books are used by first-time homeowners, seasoned investors, and financial professionals seeking a clearer, more honest understanding of how modern lending really works.

Joseph created *The Home Equity Wealth Series* to give everyday homeowners the same financial knowledge that banks, hedge funds, and institutional investors use to control capital and minimize risk. His mission is simple: to help people stop guessing, stop fearing debt, and start using smart leverage to build real financial freedom.

When he is not structuring loans or writing, Joseph works with families and investors across the United States to design personalized equity strategies that align with their goals, cash flow, and long-term wealth plans.

The Home Equity Wealth Series Roadmap

The Professional Guide to Using Your Home to Build Financial Freedom

The purpose of *The Home Equity Wealth Series* is to give homeowners the same financial tools and strategies used by banks, investors, and institutions—translated into clear, practical guidance for everyday people. Each book builds on the last, taking you from basic understanding to advanced mastery of how to use home equity safely, intelligently, and profitably across every stage of life.

Book 1 — *HELOC Fundamentals*This book gives you the foundation. You will understand how Home Equity Lines of Credit work, how they are structured, how risk is controlled, and how equity becomes usable capital. The books that follow are designed to help you apply that knowledge to your own situation, your income type, your credit profile, and your long-term financial goals.

Book 2 — *How to Qualify for a HELOC* This book shows you how lenders actually evaluate borrowers. You will learn how credit scores, income, property type, and debt ratios affect approval, limits, and interest rates. You will also learn how to position yourself to qualify for the largest possible credit line at the best possible terms.

Book 3 — *HELOCs for Real Estate Investors* This book focuses on using home equity to buy, rehab, refinance, and scale rental properties. It explains how investors use HELOCs for down payments, renovations, and portfolio growth while keeping cash flow positive and risk controlled.

Book 4 — *Self-Employed HELOC Strategies* Designed for business owners, freelancers, 1099 borrowers, and LLCs, this book explains how bank-statement income, business income, and alternative documentation can be used to qualify for home equity even when traditional tax returns do not reflect true cash flow.

Book 5 — *Credit Mastery for HELOC Approval* This book dives deep into credit strategy. You will learn how utilization, credit mix, and reporting behavior affect HELOC limits and pricing—and how to optimize your credit profile specifically for home equity approval.

Book 6 — *No-Doc & Alternative HELOC Programs* This book covers asset-based HELOCs, no-income-verification options, and non-traditional lending programs for high-net-worth, self-employed, or cash-heavy borrowers who do not fit inside standard underwriting models.

Book 7 — *Using a HELOC to Eliminate Debt* This book teaches how to use home equity to replace high-interest credit cards, personal loans, and auto loans with low-interest revolving credit, allowing borrowers to eliminate debt years faster and save tens of thousands of dollars in interest.

Book 8 — *Using a HELOC to Build Wealth* This book shows how homeowners fund investments, businesses, and passive income streams using HELOCs while maintaining liquidity and controlling risk.

Book 9 — *HELOC Risk Management* This book focuses entirely on safety. You will learn how to structure buffers, cash-flow coverage, rate protection, and leverage limits so your home becomes safer over time—not more vulnerable.

Book 10 — *The Smart Borrower's Home Equity Blueprint* The final book ties everything together into a complete lifetime strategy for using home equity as a personal banking system, investment engine, and financial safety net.

Book 11 — *The Cashflow Accelerator Method*

The Cashflow Accelerator Method is the final transformation stage of *The Home Equity Wealth Series*. While the earlier books teach how to access, qualify for, and safely use home equity, this book teaches how to **weaponize cash flow itself** to permanently eliminate debt and create lasting wealth. Together, these books are designed to turn a single asset—your home—into a lifelong financial advantage. Each volume adds another layer of understanding, allowing you to move from homeowner to capital manager, from borrower to strategist, and from financial stress to long-term stability.

This is not about taking more risk.It is about learning how money really works—and using that knowledge to build financial freedom that lasts.

Educational & Financial Disclaimer

This book is provided for **educational and informational purposes only**. The author and publisher are not engaged in rendering legal, tax, accounting, investment, or financial advice. Although the author is a licensed mortgage broker, the information in this book is intended to provide general education about Home Equity Lines of Credit (HELOCs) and home equity strategy, not personalized financial, legal, or lending advice.

Mortgage programs, underwriting guidelines, interest rates, credit requirements, and home equity products vary by lender, investor, state, and economic conditions, and may change at any time without notice. The examples, calculations, and scenarios presented in this book are hypothetical and are for illustration only. They do not represent guaranteed outcomes or actual loan approvals.

Before making any financial decisions, including applying for a HELOC, refinancing, borrowing against home equity, or using credit for investment or debt repayment, readers should consult with a qualified mortgage professional, financial advisor, tax advisor, or attorney who can evaluate their specific situation.

Risk Disclosure

Borrowing against home equity involves risk. A HELOC is secured by your home, which means failure to make required payments could result in foreclosure or loss of property. This book teaches responsible, conservative, and structured use of home equity, but no financial strategy is risk-free.

Readers are solely responsible for their financial decisions. Neither the author nor the publisher makes any warranties, express or implied, about the accuracy, completeness, or applicability of the information in this book to any individual or situation.

www.ingramcontent.com/pod-product-compliance
Ingram Content Group UK Ltd.
Pitfield, Milton Keynes, MK11 3LW, UK
UKHW020157290926
15471UKWH00005B/927

9 798295 574207